Holocaust

by
Daniel P. Cusenza & Merle Davenport

Cover Graphics by
Vickie Lane

Inside Illustrations by
Pat Biggs

Cover Photo
Corbis-Bettmann

Publisher
Instructional Fair • TS Denison
Grand Rapids, Michigan 49544

Permission to Reproduce

Instructional Fair • TS Denison grants the right to the individual purchaser to reproduce patterns and student activity materials in this book for noncommercial individual or classroom use only. Reproduction for an entire school or school system is strictly prohibited. No other part of this publication may be reproduced in whole or in part. No part of this publication may be reproduced for storage in a retrieval system, or transmitted in any form or by any means, electronic, mechanical, recording, or otherwise, without the prior written permission of the publisher. For information regarding permission write to: Instructional Fair • TS Denison, P.O. Box 1650, Grand Rapids, MI 49501.

Credits

Authors: Daniel P. Cusenza
Merle Davenport
Cover Graphics: Vickie Lane
Inside Illustrations: Pat Biggs
Project Director/Editor: Sharon Kirkwood
Editors: Lisa Hancock, Rhonda DeWaard
Production: Pat Geasler, Vickie Lane

Photos   Corbis–Bettmann
UPI/Corbis–Bettmann
Reuters/Corbis–Bettmann

Standard Book Number: 1-56822-453-2
Holocaust
Copyright © 1997 by Instructional Fair • TS Denison
2400 Turner Avenue NW
Grand Rapids, Michigan 49544
All Rights Reserved • Printed in the USA

Table of Contents

History can be thought of as a map to the lessons learned by society over the ages. Like any good map, the danger signs often are clearly defined. Unfortunately, the signs are often ignored or forgotten in society's haste to step into the future. As a result, harsh new lessons are learned and mistakes are repeated. Some mistakes have been repeated far too many times. Genocide is one such mistake. Humans can work against this cycle of violence by learning how the past bears on the future.

There are hundreds of examples in history involving genocide based on religion, race, culture, geographic location, and many other reasons. One example of butchery stands out from the rest—the mass murder of the Jews by Nazi Germany during World War II, otherwise known as the *Holocaust.*

To attempt to catalogue the horrendous acts perpetrated against Jews and other "undesirables" during the Nazi regime would take up volumes of text. Thus, the focus of this book is to use specific events and ideas to highlight and give a sense of the atrocities committed.

Much of the information in this book is meant to promote class discussion and to draw analogies that students can relate to on a more personal level. The sheer immensity of facts and statistics are numbing but do not convey the "human element." Yet it is on the human level that these lessons must be remembered and incorporated into one's life experience.

Due to the serious and graphic nature of the subject, it is best to notify students' parents or guardians of the curriculum to be discussed. It is also recommended that parents/guardians be encouraged to talk with their children and to help answer any questions the students may pose.

The challenges of conveying the appalling events of the Holocaust are many. They are not, however, insurmountable. Rising to the challenge requires patience but will be rewarding for you and the students.

The Eye on History series strives to bring history to life through the personal experiences of those who lived them. The letters, diary accounts, postcards, and so on are fictitious. However, the facts contained in them represent what individuals might have written. The more students are able to experience history through what others may have felt and thought, the more meaningful it will be. After all, history is not just musty dates and facts. History is the stories of individuals and nations and of heroes and ordinary people. It is influenced by fashions and passions. We hope this series will help students understand history in new and exciting ways.

Why Study the Holocaust?

   Record your thoughts and knowledge about the Holocaust by answering the questions. Try to be as honest as you can. Your teacher may decide to repeat this exercise at the end of your study of the Holocaust.

What is your understanding of the Holocaust? _____

_____

_____

_____

Do you believe we should study the Holocaust? Explain. _____

_____

_____

_____

What do you expect to learn by studying the Holocaust? _____

_____

_____

_____

What is your understanding of discrimination or prejudice? _____

_____

_____

_____

Do you believe there are ways to stop discrimination or prejudice? Explain.

_____

_____

_____

What might you do to stop discrimination or prejudice? _____

_____

_____

_____

How do you believe studying the Holocaust will change you? _____

_____

_____

_____

Additional thoughts: _____

_____

_____

The Chronicle Herald

April 1945

Americans Liberate Dachau Concentration Camp

DACHAU, Germany—American soldiers were greeted today by the hollow faces of the prisoners as they liberated the Nazi concentration camp located at Dachau, Germany. The scene spoke of the horrors humans are capable of if unrestrained by conscience. Rumors had circulated for many years of the unspeakable tortures inflicted on the Jews and other political prisoners. However, the reality of these conditions was far worse than anyone had imagined. Gaunt faces with little more than pale skin stretched over bone saw their first glimmer of freedom. Many prisoners were so emaciated that they may not survive.

In the background stand the brick ovens that were used to reduce the bodies of the dead to ashes. They are silent now as they bear quiet testimony to the horrors committed. Prisoners were denied the basic necessities of adequate food and clothing, medical attention, sanitary living conditions, and even personal identity. The Nazis had reduced them to the numbers tattooed on their arms.

Many prisoners died of disease. Others died of exhaustion, starvation, or as a result of torturous medical experimentation. There are rumors that other camps contained gas chambers to murder the Jews. There was no need for gas chambers here. The conditions of the camp were murderous enough. The filth in the overcrowded camp was a perfect breeding ground for vermin. Anyone too weak or exhausted to work was eliminated. There was no room in the camp for those who could not contribute.

Yet the question remains, "Why didn't we know of these terrible deeds?" Perhaps some of our leaders had heard but could not bring themselves to believe that anyone would attempt to wipe out an entire group of people. Many wild rumors circulate during the course of war. This one may have been beyond belief.

Perhaps the world will never know the exact number of lives carelessly discarded by the Nazis. Perhaps the true extent of the tortures will never be discovered. But let us never forget what we have witnessed here, lest we allow it to happen again.

Many soldiers were unprepared for what they found at the concentration camps. The horror of what they saw was beyond comprehension. As part of your study of the Holocaust, keep a journal of your thoughts. Address such questions as: What did you learn? How can you apply the lessons of the Holocaust to today? What can you do to stop the hate and prejudice that leads to situations such as the Holocaust? Why do you think the Holocaust happened? How can we prevent it from happening again?

My Holocaust Journal

_____

_____

_____

_____

_____

_____

_____

_____

_____

_____

_____

_____

_____

_____

_____

_____

_____

_____

_____

_____

_____

_____

Note: By no means is this chronology meant to be a definitive list of events of the Holocaust. Feel free to add additional items during your study.

1933

January 30 — Adolf Hitler is appointed Reich's Chancellor (Prime Minister) by President Hindenburg.

March 20 — Establishment of the first German concentration camp at Dachau.

April 1 — Boycott of Jewish shops and businesses.

May 10 — Public burning of books written by Jews and opponents of Nazism.

Spring/ Summer — Jewish professors are expelled from the universities, and Jewish writers and artists are prohibited from pursuing their work.

July — Law passes that revokes citizenship of German Jews naturalized since 1918.

October 4 — Editor–Law excludes all Jewish editors from work.

1935

May 21 — "Aryan Heritage" becomes a mandatory prerequisite for military service.

"Jews Not Wanted" signs begin to appear on restaurants, businesses, and public notice boards.

May 31 — Jews are barred from military service.

September 14 — The Nuremberg Laws are passed, revoking the citizenship of all German Jews.

November 14 — All Jews lose the right to vote and hold public office.

All Jewish children are restricted from using the same playgrounds and locker rooms as other children.

1937

January — Aryanization of the economy begins as Jewish business people are forced to sell, usually at a severe loss.

July 16 — Concentration camp at Buchenwald is opened.

1938

March — Persecution of Austrian Jews following the annexation of Austria.

June 15 — All "previously convicted" Jews are arrested and sent to concentration camps.

July 28 — Medical certification of Jewish physicians is revoked.

September 12 — Jews are prohibited from attending public cultural events.

September 27 — Jewish attorneys have their licenses cancelled.

October 5 — Jewish passports are recalled and marked with a "J."

Nov. 9-10 — *Kristallnacht* (Night of the Broken Glass), a government-organized, anti-Semitic program that involved the destruction of synagogues and businesses.

November 12 — Jews are forced to relinquish control of all retail shops to Aryans.

November 15 — Jewish children are expelled from German schools.

November 28 — Police limit the movement of Jews in public.

December 8 — Jews are no longer allowed to attend the universities.

Continued on page 9.

Continued from page 8.

1939

January 30	Hitler threatens extermination of all European Jews if war breaks out.
September 1	Curfew is established for German Jews.
	Germany attacks Poland. WWII begins.
September 17	Eastern Poland is invaded and occupied by Soviets.
September 23	Confiscation of radios from Jews.

1940

February 12	German Jews are deported to concentration camps in Lublin, Poland.
April 27	Himmler orders the construction of a concentration camp at Auschwitz.

1941

February 22	400 Dutch Jews are sent to the concentration camp Mauthausen. Dutch workers strike in protest.
April 4	The murder of the "handicapped" in concentration camps begins.
June–Dec.	Nazi *Einsatzgruppen* (mobile killing units) massacre Jews in German-occupied Soviet territories.
July 31	Göring assigns Heydrich to implement the "Final Solution."
September 1	All Jews must wear the Yellow Star in areas occupied by Nazis.
September 28	34,000 Jews are murdered at Babi Yar near Kiev.
October 14	Mass deportation of Jews to concentration camps begins.
December 8	Nazi soldiers at Chelmno, the first concentration camp built exclusively for the extermination of humans, begin gassing prisoners.

1942

March 1	Jews are exterminated by gas at Sobibor.
March 17	Jews are gassed at Belzec.
July 4	Mass gassing begins at Auschwitz in the "new and improved" gas chambers.
July 19	Himmler orders extermination of Jews in occupied Poland be completed by the end of December 1942.

1943

January 20	Camp doctors give orders that sick and debilitated prisoners are to be killed.
May 26	In order to hide the number of deaths occurring in the camps, a secret numbering code is established.
October 2	Some 7,220 Danish Jews and German Jewish refugees are saved from deportation by the Danish underground.

1944

November 26	Himmler orders the destruction of the crematoriums at Auschwitz to hide the evidence of the death camps.

1945

January 17	The "Death March" from Auschwitz begins.
April 11	American troops liberate Buchenwald.
April 28	Austrian prisoners are the last to be sent to the gas chambers in Mauthausen.
April 28	Dachau is liberated by Americans.
April 30	Hitler commits suicide.

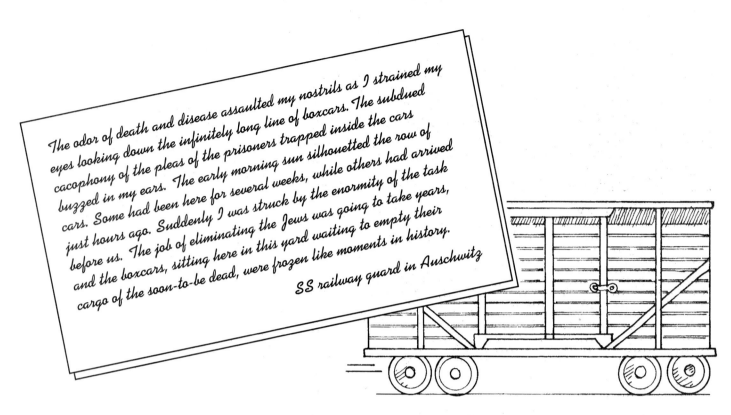

The odor of death and disease assaulted my nostrils as I strained my eyes looking down the infinitely long line of boxcars. The subdued cacophony of the pleas of the prisoners trapped inside the cars buzzed in my ears. The early morning sun silhouetted the row of cars. Some had been here for several weeks, while others had arrived just hours ago. Suddenly I was struck by the enormity of the task before us. The job of eliminating the Jews was going to take years, and the boxcars, sitting here in this yard waiting to empty their cargo of the soon-to-be dead, were frozen like moments in history.

SS railway guard in Auschwitz

Imagine yourself being transported several hundred miles in a filled-to-capacity cattle car or boxcar, with no idea of your destination. The trip could last a few hours or a number of days.

On the lines below, describe in vivid detail what the experience might be like. Describe the sights, the sounds, and the smells, as well as the diverse group of people with whom you are traveling.

_____

_____

_____

_____

_____

_____

_____

_____

_____

_____

_____

November 11, 1938
Munich, Germany

Dear Catherine,

I am taking this opportunity to write as I dare not go outside. Last night there was rioting in the Jewish quarter. Mobs surged through the streets destroying shops and homes. Angry voices filled the air while glass shattered all around. This is the worst demonstration of hatred against the Jews thus far. I do not understand why they are so hated. Our neighbor Herr Goldstein won several medals fighting for Germany in World War I. Now he is treated as an enemy of the very country he fought so hard to defend. In fact, his house was damaged in the rampage along with other Jewish shops, businesses, and synagogues. The door was shattered, graffiti was scrawled across the walls, and every window was broken.

As I said, I dare not go outside. There are spies watching to see who assists the Jews in cleaning up. If I am seen helping the Jews, they may carry me off like other Jewish sympathizers. I hope things change soon.

Carla

Kristallnacht (Night of the Broken Glass) was about 48 hours of anti-Jewish rioting all across Germany. Gangs of thugs organized by the government destroyed and looted homes, businesses, and synagogues. Thousands of Jews were seized and shipped to concentration camps. Numerous synagogues were destroyed and an estimated 7,500 shops were ransacked. In addition, Jews were ordered to restore the storefronts at their own expense. They were also forced to raise about 1 billion marks as an "atonement payment" to the government. This night, more than any other, marked the official persecution of the Jews and is considered the beginning of the Holocaust in 1938.

Imagine that your home or business was attacked during *Kristallnacht.* You must clean up the mess. Place some of the articles you find in an imaginary box and list why you consider them significant. For example, broken glass symbolizes the violence of discrimination; a broken toy demonstrates how children are innocent victims of hatred; a broken table leg signifies the table where the family gathered for evening meals; a Star of David symbolizes the religious devotion that the Nazis found so offensive.

Kristallnacht Reminder: _____

Significance of Reminder: _____

Kristallnacht Reminder: _____

Significance of Reminder: _____

Kristallnacht Reminder: _____

Significance of Reminder: _____

April 18, 1941

Dear Diary,

Well, it has been another risky day. German soldiers are everywhere. I went shopping for dinner today and felt the cold stare of German spies everywhere. Perhaps I am just nervous because Papa is helping Jews escape to America. The worst part is that most of the spies are friends and neighbors who wish to gain favor with the Nazi occupation. Many even sell out family members for small rewards. I am convinced we are doing the right thing by helping the Jews. I don't understand what they have done to deserve Nazi wrath. But then, who ever understands the ways of hatred?

Franz was following me today. I know that he did not know I saw him. He checked with each shopkeeper to make sure I did not buy more than our family needs for supper. He must suspect that we are hiding Jews. Papa hopes that we will be able to leave soon. He thinks someone at work suspects him. If we are not caught first, we will leave quietly in the middle of the night as others have. Rumor has it that enemies of the Nazis are taken to special prisons called concentration camps where the prisoners are forced to work long hours. Most die within months due to starvation or disease.

I must stop before the spies see my candle burning too late at night. I must also be careful to hide this diary where the Nazis can't find it in case they search our house.

The hatred the Nazis had for Jews was untempered by mercy. Nazis were taught that loyalty to duty was the most important virtue. This included carrying out the orders of their superiors, especially Hitler, without question. Anyone caught helping the Jews was considered an enemy of the state. They were usually arrested in the middle of the night and taken to a concentration camp. The Gestapo (Nazi secret police) encouraged people to turn in friends, neighbors, parents, or other family members suspected of disloyalty.

The Gestapo would search homes of suspected Jewish sympathizers without warning, and would destroy their business or even hold family members hostage to ensure cooperation. For those with enough courage to resist, the disease, forced labor, and appalling conditions of the concentration camps often resulted in death. For others, the threat of being sent to the camps kept them from helping the Jews or protesting the methods of the Gestapo.

Use with page 12.

Discuss . . .

- why the Nazis would rely on spies and secret police to enforce their anti-Jewish policies.
- how life under Gestapo rule would differ from life in a society in which you are innocent until proven guilty.
- whether you would have been bold enough to help Jews escape.
- ways (such as buying extra food) neighbors might become suspicious that you were helping Jews to escape.
- what you would need (such as fake passports) to help Jews escape.

For Further Study

- How was the work of Jewish sympathizers similar to or different from the Underground Railroad in the United States?
- How was the status of the American slave similar to or different from that of the German Jew?
- Compare the Nazi Gestapo to the KGB of the Soviet Union.
- Compare the Nazi concentration camps to the Siberian labor camps.

Concentration Camps

The map on page 15 shows the locations of the eighteen primary concentration camps established by the Nazis. Also indicated are the six extermination camps that were established for the exclusive purpose of killing Jews. This includes the notorious Auschwitz. Soldiers of that camp alone were responsible for the deaths of over 2.5 million people.

Using a resource from the period under study, label the following countries on the map on page 15. After doing further reading, proceed with the discussion below.

Norway	Greece	Italy	Bulgaria
U.S.S.R.	Austria	France	Romania
Luxembourg	Poland	Hungary	Denmark
Yugoslavia	Germany	Belgium	Estonia
Lithuania	Netherlands	Czechoslovakia	Latvia
East Prussia	Finland	Switzerland	Sweden
Albania	Turkey		

Discuss . . .

- why Hitler would locate the death camps outside of Germany.
- why the concentration camps (often used for forced labor) would be concentrated mostly in Germany.
- why Poland was chosen as the site for most of the death camps.
- why camps were not located in Italy, Hungary, or Romania.

For Further Study

- Compare Germany's concentration camps to the U.S.'s internment of Japanese Americans.
- Why was there so little resistance to the creation and use of death camps?
- Nazi Germany had an alliance with the Soviet Union. Why did they break it and kill millions of Soviet citizens?

Vaivara
Klooga
Stutthof
Neuengamme
Ravensbrück
Bergen-Belsen
Sachsenhausen
Treblinka
Chelmno
Mittelbau Dora
Gross Rosen
Sobibor
Buchenwald
Majdanek
Auschwitz
Flossenberg
Plaszow
Belzec
Natzweiler
Dachau
Mauthausen
Jasenovac
Gospic
Sajmiste

Extermination Camps
Concentration Camps

Listed below are several terms that are frequently used when studying the events of the Holocaust. Use the vocabulary terms to complete the *Vocabulary Match-Ups* exercises on page 17.

Anti-Semitism—Discrimination or persecution of Jews.

Appelplatz—Roll call area inside concentration, labor, and death camps.

Aryan—Racial term used by Nazis to describe a "race" they believed to be superior. It has no biological validity.

Bericha—Hebrew for "flight"; name given to those who aided Jews in their escape to Palestine after the Holocaust.

Concentration Camp—Place where political prisoners were kept.

Crematorium—Furnaces where human bodies were burned.

Deportation—The forced removal of Jews in Nazi-occupied lands to concentration camps.

Death Camps—Nazi centers of murder and extermination.

Death Marches—The marches imposed upon prisoners by the Nazis in order to keep them from liberation by the Allied forces.

Einsatzgruppen—SS killing units that sought out and slaughtered Jews in the Soviet Union.

Euthanasia—The policy of "mercy killing" the old and handicapped.

Final Solution—The Nazi term for the annihilation of the Jews in Europe.

Genocide—The systematic elimination of a people or nation.

Gestapo—Abbreviation for *Geheime Staatspolizei* (Secret State Police).

Ghetto—The section of a city where Jews were forced to live.

Holocaust—Term used to refer to the systematic murder of 6 million Jews by the Nazis between 1933 and 1945. Also included extermination of Gypsies and Poles.

Juden—German for "Jews."

Judenrat—Head of the Jewish council established by the Nazis in each Jewish ghetto.

Judenrein—German term that means "pure" or "clean" of Jews.

Kristallnacht—"Night of the Broken Glass." Nazi-organized riot against the Jews on Nov. 9–10, 1938.

Nazi—Acronym for the National Socialist German Workers Party.

Pogroms—Organized acts of persecution or massacre of a specific group of people.

Prejudice—An *attitude* toward a person or group of people formed without adequate information.

Racism—*Practice* of discrimination and persecution on the basis of race.

Scapegoat—An innocent person blamed for the problems of another.

Selection—The procedure used to determine who would live and who would die in death and labor camps. Usually carried out by doctors.

Swastika—Symbol of the Nazi party; originally an ancient religious symbol.

Uebermenschen—Nazi term for "supermen," the racial ideal.

Yellow Star—Yellow, cloth Star of David sewn to clothing to identify Jews.

Zyklon-B—The gas used to kill Jews in the gas chambers at the death camps.

Vocabulary Match-Ups

Use the vocabulary from page 16 to match each definition with its corresponding term. Write the appropriate letter beside each term.

Part I

_____ 1. Ghetto

_____ 2. Racism

_____ 3. Crematorium

_____ 4. Deportation

_____ 5. Selection

_____ 6. *Bericha*

_____ 7. *Judenrat*

_____ 8. Genocide

_____ 9. *Uebermenschen*

_____ 10. Anti-Semitism

A. Head of Jewish council established by the Nazis in each ghetto.

B. The forced removal of Jews in Nazi-occupied lands to concentration camps.

C. The section of a city in which the Jews were forced to live.

D. Nazi term for "supermen," the racial ideal.

E. Procedure used to determine who would live and who would die in death and labor camps. Usually carried out by doctors.

F. Furnaces where human bodies were burned.

G. Discrimination or persecution of Jews.

H. The practice of discrimination and persecution on the basis of race.

I. The systematic elimination of a people or nation.

J. Hebrew for "flight"; name given to those who aided the Jews in their escape to Palestine after the Holocaust.

Part II

_____ 1. Gestapo

_____ 2. *Appelplatz*

_____ 3. Holocaust

_____ 4. Pogroms

_____ 5. Nazi

_____ 6. *Kristallnacht*

_____ 7. *Juden*

_____ 8. Death Camps

_____ 9. Zyklon-B

_____ 10. Final Solution

A. The gas used to kill Jews in the gas chambers of Auschwitz.

B. "Night of the Broken Glass." Nazi-organized riot against the Jews.

C. Organized acts of persecution or massacre of a specific group of people.

D. Secret police.

E. Roll call area inside concentration, labor, and death camps.

F. Term used to refer to the systematic murder of 6 million Jews by Nazis between 1933 and 1945.

G. German for "Jews."

H. The Nazi term for the annihilation of the Jews of Europe.

I. Acronym for the National Socialist German Workers Party.

J. Nazi centers for murder and extermination.

Part III

_____ 1. Prejudice

_____ 2. *Einsatzgruppen*

_____ 3. Scapegoat

_____ 4. Swastika

_____ 5. Concentration Camp

_____ 6. Death Marches

_____ 7. Aryan

_____ 8. Yellow Star

_____ 9. Euthanasia

_____ 10. *Judenrein*

A. The policy of "mercy killing" the elderly and the handicapped.

B. Cloth Star of David sewn on clothing to identify Jews.

C. An attitude toward a person or group of people formed without adequate information.

D. "Pure" or "clean" of Jews.

E. An innocent person blamed for the problems of another.

F. The Nazis considered this the "superior race."

G. SS killing units that sought out and murdered Jews in the Soviet Union.

H. Forced marches to keep prisoners from being liberated by the Allies.

I. Place where political prisoners were kept.

J. Symbol of the Nazi party.

> *May 1943*
>
> *It is night now. I do not know if the Germans will attack again or not. They came prepared to find a weak, submissive population willing to be transported to their deaths. Instead, they found stout resistance. There are not enough guns for all of us, so we must fight with whatever we can find. We have fought them in the streets and in the sewers. If it were possible, we would fight them after death. Like King David of old, we are not afraid of this Goliath in a German uniform.*

The Warsaw Ghetto uprising marked the first and only example of Jewish resistance to Hitler's designs. By late 1940, the Nazis had sealed off about 400,000 Jews into an old medieval district of Warsaw, Poland, that normally housed 160,000 people. The high wall they built around the ghetto assured the Germans that the Jews would not escape.

The Germans allotted only enough food to sustain half of the population. Many survived on a bowl of soup a day. This soup was often made of boiled straw. However, the Warsaw Jews did not die of starvation quickly enough to satisfy Himmler, the chief of the German police, so he ordered their removal and extermination.

On July 22, 1942, the "resettlement" of the Jews began. By October 3, over 300,000 had been sent to death camps to be gassed. When Himmler visited the Warsaw Ghetto in January 1943, he was surprised to discover that there were still 60,000 Jews living there. He ordered their removal by February 15. However, Germany's defeat at Stalingrad forced the Germans to focus on and send additional equipment to the Russian front instead. As a result, it was not until April 19 that Germany was able to turn its attention to Warsaw.

The Nazis advanced on the Ghetto with over 2,000 men equiped with tanks, flame throwers, artillery, and demolition squads into an area measuring only 1,000 x 300 yards. The Jews had used the extra time to honeycomb the ghetto with fortified positions and gather an odd assortment of pistols, rifles, a few machine guns, and homemade grenades.

For four weeks, the determined Jews held off the Germans. They fought in the streets, the alleys, the basements, and on rooftops. When the Germans systematically destroyed the buildings of the ghetto, the few remaining Jews hid in the woods and sewers. Finally, on May 16, the Germans declared the rebellion crushed. Over 56,000 had resisted. They preferred to fight and die for freedom rather than be shipped to the death camps.

Discuss . . .

- how ghettoization enabled Warsaw Jews to organize.
- why these Jews preferred to fight to the death.
- why you believe other Jews did not or were not able to resist.
- what lessons we can learn from the example of the Warsaw Jews.

Extension

- Write a descriptive paragraph of what life might have been like in the Warsaw Ghetto.

When the German army invaded Denmark in the spring of 1940, they met with little resistance from the Danes. Thus, the Danish government was allowed to keep its autonomy. However, when they were told to implement anti-Semitic policies, they refused.

The Danish people showed their selflessness to the world by unifying to protect the Danish Jews. Hitler's decree, in the autumn of 1943, that all the Danish Jews be sent to Auschwitz was a rallying cry for the Danish people. From the armed forces all the way down to the local police departments, not a single Dane would cooperate. They refused to round up the approximately 6,500 Danes who were Jewish and the 800 German Jewish refugees.

Nor was it the Danes alone who felt that the injustice against the Jews must not be propagated in Denmark. General Von Hanneken, the German Army Commander, refused to use his troops for the purpose of gathering up the Jews. He successfully argued that it was not the way his troops were meant to be used. Eventually, SS troops had to be sent from Germany.

When the SS tried to round up the Jews, the situation was different from others the Gestapo had encountered. Now they had Danish law to contend with: forced entry and the abduction of residents was illegal. Since the Danish government was still in power, it had the ability to enforce those laws. Armed resistance was promised if the SS broke any of these laws. As a result, the SS was forced to go from door to door. If no one answered, they were to continue on to the next home. Of the 7,220 Jews in Denmark, only 477 were taken on that particular night.

The Swedish government agreed to grant sanctuary to the Danish Jews. This started a mass mobilization of resources in Denmark to get the Jews to this safe haven. A Danish fishing fleet was employed to move the Jews from Denmark to Sweden. The citizens raised money to pay for the escapees' passage. The police warded off dangers, while pharmacists supplied stimulants to keep people on the move throughout the nighttime efforts. The Jews were often taken to the "vehicle of deliverance" in taxi cabs to fend off suspicions. Before the month was over, the Danish people had managed to rescue thousands of Jews, plus any non-Jewish spouses. Such selfless efforts of the Danes on behalf of the Jewish community demonstrates a strength of character that is both admirable and heart-warming.

Discuss . . .

- why you think the Danes refused to help Hitler destroy the Jews.

- why General Von Hanneken refused to obey Hitler's orders.

- why the SS had no authority to round up Jews in Denmark.

- the fact that in the fall of 1943, Hitler was losing the war on all fronts. Do you think this influenced his decision not to attack Denmark for its defiance? Explain.

- whether you think the Holocaust would have happened if all countries had resisted Hitler's policies the way the Danes did.

It was during Hanukkah in 1941. Our section of the hospital block was called to march in front of our Nazi masters. Anyone too sick or weak had their number taken; we all knew that this meant they were to be executed. The rest of us, over two thousand, were forced to parade naked in front of the German officers. Those who were young and pretty were herded into another room. We did not want to imagine what their fate might be. The rest of us had our numbers taken. We were terrified. They led us back to our block where we stayed until the next day, when we were loaded into trucks and driven to another part of the camp. Many were crying and clinging to each other.

The trucks stopped in front of a large building where we were ordered to undress and enter the showers for delousing. Towels were hanging on hooks on the walls; some toiletries and mirrors were available. We were crowded so tightly into the shower that we barely had room to move. This was when I knew they were going to kill us. Many of the women were shouting at each other, crying, and even hitting one another. Healthy and sick, strong and weak, young and old were all packed together in that room. Suddenly, my eyes watered and I began to cough violently. My throat felt as if it had closed off completely. We all crumpled to the floor trying to cling to life.

I do not remember the door opening, but I heard my name being called. I could not answer, so I weakly raised my arm. Rough hands pulled me from the room and allowed me my first gasps of fresh air. Someone threw a blanket around me and took me to the hospital. I remained hospitalized for several weeks before I was taken to the political department. It was then explained to me that a mistake had been made. I should not have been sent to the gas chamber because my husband was a Polish officer.

Use with page 20.

There were three camps that comprised Auschwitz. Each had its own purpose. Auschwitz I was a camp for political prisoners and criminals. Auschwitz II-Birkenau was the extermination camp, and Auschwitz III-Monowitz was where slave labor was enlisted to build a synthetic rubber plant. In addition, there were 35 satellite labors camps in a 50-mile radius.

Cattle cars, crammed with people, would arrive regularly at Auschwitz II-Birkenau. The people would be forced from the cars and lined up for an immediate selection. They were separated according to how productive they might be. Children under sixteen and those over forty, the handicapped, and mothers with infants were automatically deemed "non-productive" and sent to the gas chambers. The men and doctors who made these decisions would simply look at the person before them and flick their wrist to indicate which side to step to. One line meant one's life would be prolonged for a short time; the other meant immediate death.

Those who survived this selection process were sent to Auschwitz III-Monowitz or to one of the smaller camps as slave laborers. Some were sent to work in the crematoriums and gas chambers, while others were given kitchen or latrine duty. Most of those still alive were killed after three months to allow "fresh" workers to take over. Skilled or educated people were spared for a time as well, providing the SS had an immediate need for them.

The SS doctors gave careful consideration to determining the level and type of rations given to the prisoners. The developing malnutrition, as a result of these rations, was timed to kill a prisoner in three months. Thus, many prisoners were forced to take from those around them in order to survive.

Auschwitz II-Birkenau was equipped with four gas chambers that had the capacity to murder 15,000 people a day. When the advancing Russian army forced Auschwitz to be abandoned in 1944, an estimated three million had met their deaths in Auschwitz. Of those slaughtered, two and a half million were Jews.

Discuss . . .

- why you think the Germans used numbers for the prisoners instead of names.
- why you think it made a difference that the woman in the "eyewitness" account on page 20 was saved because she was married to a Polish officer.
- why the Nazis would try to disguise the true purpose of the showers by equipping them with towels and mirrors.
- the fact that before the invention of Zyklon-B gas, most prisoners were killed by bullets, starvation, or exhaust fumes from specially designed trucks. Why do you think the Nazis preferred to use the gas chambers?
- the fact that as the Soviet army approached Auschwitz, the Germans abandoned the camp, yet forced the prisoners to march to a new location. Why do you think the Germans didn't simply kill all the prisoners before abandoning the camp?
- why you think the prisoners didn't fight back.
- why you think the Germans used the money and resources to create and run death camps, when they needed those same resources to fight the Allies.

> Dear Diary,
>   I do not know if anyone will ever read these words. I write them with the hope that someday the world may know the truth of our existence within the camp of Auschwitz-Birkenau. The hospital wards are quarantine buildings, each housing up to a thousand women. Each building is dedicated to prisoners with a specific disease. I am housed in the one for tuberculosis. My friend Ruth is in the one for dysentery. There are separate buildings for typhus, scarlet fever, diphtheria, and a host of other diseases. The conditions in the camp seem to be a healthy place for diseases, if not for humans. There is no medicine, but some with medical training try to keep our spirits up.
>   The main duty of the hospital workers is not to heal, but to cart away the bodies of the dead. I have heard that as many as five to six hundred a day are carried to the crematoriums. I know that I have seen more death here in the past few weeks than anyone should see in a lifetime. It is truly hard to believe that with so much death, there is still overcrowding due to new arrivals.
>   I pray that God will hear the cries of his children and rescue us soon.

The SS, always conscious of efficiency, made the most of mother nature's unwitting assistance. Rather than waste money on gas, or even more valuable bullets, they separated the sick from the healthy and let the sick die. Sometimes the demand for space became so great that the ill prisoners were loaded aboard trucks and shipped to the crematoriums alive.

Part I

Reread the diary entry above. Imagine what life might have been like in Auschwitz. What might you have eaten? Where might you have slept? How might you have been treated by the guards? What might you do to pass the time? Record these thoughts, plus any others into your diary. Use another page, if necessary.

Dear Diary,

_____

_____

_____

_____

_____

_____

_____

_____

Natural Killers

Use with page 22.

Part II

Fill in the following chart. You may wish to contact your physician, your county health department, or the U.S. Center for Disease Control in Atlanta, Georgia, for information. After completing the chart, discuss why you think diseases such as these ran rampant among the prisoners.

Disease	Definition	Causes	Symptoms	Prevention
Cholera				
Diphtheria				
Dysentery				
Smallpox				
Scarlet Fever				
Tuberculosis				
Typhus				

© Instructional Fair • TS Denison   23   IF2665 *Holocaust*

Dearest Sally,

What I witnessed today made me weep. We were silently greeted at the gates of the concentration camp by the frail forms of men barely able to stand and too weak to speak. We may have liberated the camp today, but the horrors of what took place here will haunt these tortured souls for the rest of their lives. Never in my worst nightmares have I seen such evil. How many are dead because of the atrocities spawned by the hatred of one man? It grieves me that this man had no regard for the scores of individuals who all had their own unique stories and personalities. They were despised for one reason only: They were Jews.

Love,
David

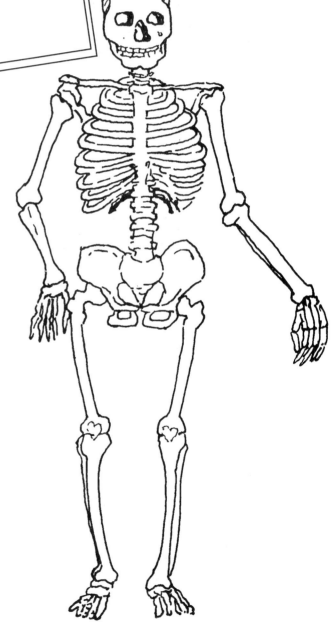

In August of 1943, 56 men and 30 women were selected to be gassed in Auschwitz. Then the flesh was stripped from their bones and the skeletons put on display in the skeleton collection at the Anatomical Institute of the University of Strasbourg. Imagine the horror of discovering these skeletons after the war.

Look at the skeleton. On the back of this paper, use your imagination to write a character synopsis based on the answers to the following questions.

1. What was the skin color of the individual?
2. What religion was the individual?
3. What was the individual's I.Q.?
4. What was the individual's political affiliation?
5. What did the individual do for a living?
6. How much money did the individual earn?
7. Was the individual an upstanding citizen?
8. Was the individual married or single?

What conclusions can be drawn about a person from looking only at a skeleton?

Hello, Gertrude,

I was so happy to receive the birthday card you sent. I wasn't sure if you were angry with me because of Karl and Father's argument. It was also the first word any of us had received since you left on the ship for America. It was a relief to hear that the company kept its promise of employment for Karl. Some of us thought that Karl's insistence that he had a job lined up in America was just a story, especially since he and Father had such harsh words over the Chancellor's ideology. Father is still angry with Karl, not because Karl disagreed with him, but because he called Father "a narrow-minded, gullible old man." I know that Karl didn't mean anything personal by the remark; he is just a very passionate person. I also know Karl well enough to know that he will not apologize for speaking his mind. I thought that you and I could play mediators and try to smooth things over. I have listened to Father discussing politics hundreds of times, so I will try to summarize his position. Karl might be persuaded to reconcile were he to better understand Father's point of view. Maybe they can find some areas of compromise.

Well, let's see, where do I begin? Part of Father's problem is frustration, because he thinks that the truth is so easy to see. He agrees with Hitler's assessment of the German people as a "superior Aryan race," and other non-Aryan peoples, particularly the Jews, as inferior. He feels that the interbreeding between "pure" Aryans and Jews or other undesirables such as Jehovah's Witnesses or Gypsies is totally unthinkable. He believes that were this to happen on a grand scale there would be a regression of the German race. Father believes also that if you look at all great cultures and civilizations of the past that have fallen, you will find that they fell due to the poisoning of the bloodlines. He further is convinced that all the great achievements in art and science are the result of the Aryan race. Thus, we must preserve this great line.

In rebuttal to Karl's humane and pacifistic views, Father says, "Hogwash!" As he puts it, "Pacifism and compassionate treatment are out of place in the greater scheme of things. For now, the mongrels and other lower orders are hiding behind a blanket of protection that they are able to exploit only because of this ploy. Pacifism and humane tendencies are acceptable only when the highest order of man has conquered the world. Then and only then can the true man indulge in such emotions."

I believe this is pretty close to what Father believes. As for me, I have learned to keep my opinions to myself. I miss you both with all my heart and hope to hear from you soon. Thank you again for the card and note.

Love, Anne

See page 26.

Dearest Anne,

I loved hearing from you. We weren't sure how well the mail service was operating. There have been some awful rumors about the state of affairs in Germany. Things were none too good when we left, and I have heard little to make me feel any more confident about the land we left. I ran into Mr. Goldstein yesterday when I went to the grocery store. I was very surprised and delighted to see him. Do you remember how he would give us piano lessons and reward us with a pastry when we played a piece without a mistake? Apparently he immigrated to the United States with his family about three weeks ago. He said that Rachel and Rita are doing well and would love to see some familiar faces. Karl and I have invited the Goldstein family to dinner this weekend.

While we were talking, Mr. Goldstein gave me some troubling reports about what is happening back home—things that have not been shown in the newsreels. He said that the state has begun to confiscate all property that is owned by Jews, that Jews have been removed from their jobs in government, and professors have lost their posts at the universities. I became worried about you and Father since Father shares a practice with Dr. Bendel. Mr. Goldstein said that when he left, Dr. Bendel had been ordered to treat only Jewish patients. How does this affect Father? This type of vilification is exactly what Father professes to support in order to preserve the good of Germany and mankind. I want you to know that we are concerned for your welfare. We went over your letter carefully. It is difficult to try to reach some common ground that Father, Karl, and, in truth, I could come to terms on, mainly because Father's thinking is flawed. It is not easy for me to say that. When you reach that point in your life when you realize your parents are people just like everyone else, there is bitter disappointment in the knowledge that they are not always right.

I don't know how to better explain our position than to tell you of this country's philosophy, which we have chosen to adopt. In order for Karl and me to become American citizens, we must pass a test on America and its history. So we have studied hard and found that what we like about America is its concept of equality. I believe the following, taken from the Declaration of Independence, best illustrates Karl's and my beliefs about our newly adopted home—"We hold these truths to be self-evident, that all men are created equal, that they are endowed by their Creator with certain unalienable Rights, that among these are Life, Liberty, and the Pursuit of Happiness."

Perhaps at the core of Father's beliefs these same feelings may reside. However, the methodology that he has used to arrive at these conclusions is in error. The end does not justify the means. And the means that Father and Hitler encourage are blatant violations of these "unalienable rights." Perhaps you can talk to Father. He respects you. We both know that you have always been the "apple of his eye."

I am sorry if this letter disappoints you, but I agree with Karl on this issue. Nevertheless, Karl said to tell you that, despite our political differences, you and Father are welcome to come and live with us. We would love to have you and to know you are safe. Karl said it is more fun to argue in person than through the mail. Seriously though, please consider his ideas carefully. Karl said that Father would have no problem opening a practice here in the United States.

I have to go now, but think carefully about what I've said.

Love, Gertrude

Use with pages 25 & 26.

Discuss . . .

- what you think is meant by the phrase "survival of the fittest."

- what is put forth as the cause of the collapse of past civilizations and cultures. Is there any validity to this belief? Explain.

- at what point Anne and Gertrude's father believes that pacifistic and humane attitudes can be adopted. Why is this a fallacy?

- whether the end **ever** justifies the means.

- knowing what the Declaration of Independence says and knowing what it means are not necessarily the same thing. What does the Declaration of Independence mean to you? Explain.

Extension

Read over the letters again carefully. Try to find a point on which Karl and his father-in-law could agree.

The world is many things, but it is not a social utopia. There are acts of barbarism and cruelty that occur every minute of every day. One of the circumstances that makes this possible is when people are unaware of crimes committed around them, as was the case of the human massacres that went on in the concentration camps. In several instances, the local population was unaware or chose to ignore the extremes to which the SS went to accomplish its objectives. The SS therefore did not fear retribution. When fear of retribution for one's actions is not a factor, any degree of abuse is possible.

Working in teams or in small groups, and using magazines, newspapers, TV reports, etc., as resources, research a modern-day atrocity or human rights violation. Some suggestions are provided below.

Use the form on page 29 to document the event and to provide as much information as you can about its causes. Then list the problems that arise as a result of the original violation and possible resolutions. Share your work with the whole class.

Recent Examples of Human Rights Violations:

- Iraqi attacks on rebel Kurds
- Protestant and Catholic relations in Northern Ireland
- Labor camps in the former Soviet Union
- Chinese prison labor used to make cheap products to compete on the global market
- Attacks on Guatemalen Indians by government-authorized death squads
- Murder of six Jesuit priests in El Salvador
- Massacre of Hutu and Tutsi civilians in Burundi and Rwanda
- "Ethnic cleansing" in Bosnia-Herzegovina

These are only a few examples of human rights violations that have occurred in various parts of the world. Watch TV newscasts, read newspapers and news magazines for more current examples.

Use with page 28.

Human Rights Violations

Names:	Date:

Sources of Information:

Location of Incident:

Violations:

Causes/Motivations:

Secondary Problems/Aftereffects:

Possible Resolutions/Reactions:

Afterthoughts on the Holocaust

You have just completed a study of the Holocaust. Record your thoughts and knowledge by answering the questions below.

How would you define the Holocaust? _____

_____

_____

_____

Why do you think we studied the Holocaust? _____

_____

_____

_____

What did you learn from your study of the Holocaust? _____

_____

_____

_____

What is your understanding of prejudice? _____

_____

_____

_____

Do you believe there are ways to stop prejudice and persecution? _____

_____

_____

_____

Do you believe we can prevent another Holocaust from happening? _____

_____

_____

_____

How do you believe your study of the Holocaust changed you? _____

_____

_____

_____

Additional thoughts: _____

_____

Reenact the Nuremberg Trials

- Have students research the trial held before an international military tribunal of 22 major Nazi figures. Students may wish to place Adolf Hitler on trial as well.

- Some people believed some of the sentences handed down were too harsh, since the victors of WWII were guilty of some of the same crimes. Do you think the trials should have taken place? Do you feel the sentences fit the crimes?

Creative Writing

Have students imagine themselves having some contact with a Jewish Ghetto. Then have them write a short story or letter, maybe even a poem or a dialogue from a viewpoint they might not otherwise have chosen. Some suggested perspectives:

- Nazi doctor who decides which people are executed and which ones will be sent to concentration camps

- German SS soldier who has orders to take someone's life

- Merchant who delivers supplies to the ghetto

- Member of the *Judenrat* (the Jewish council that ran the ghetto)

- Jewish family member living in England or America who receives news of what is happening in the ghettos

Schindler's List

Conduct in-depth class discussions after viewing the movie *Schindler's List*.

Answer Key

Concentration Camps (p. 15)

Vocabulary Match-Ups. (p. 17)

Part I	Part II	Part III
1. C	1. D	1. C
2. H	2. E	2. G
3. F	3. F	3. E
4. B	4. C	4. J
5. E	5. I	5. I
6. J	6. B	6. H
7. A	7. G	7. F
8. I	8. J	8. B
9. D	9. A	9. A
10. G	10. H	10. D

Natural Killers (p. 23)

Cholera
Definition: Acute bacterial infection
Causes: usually transmitted through the water supply
Symptoms: Severe diarrhea and loss of body fluids
Prevention: Sanitary water and food supply

Diphtheria
Definition: Acute infectious bacteria that creates lesions in the respiratory tract
Causes: direct contact with carriers of bacteria
Symptoms: Lesion in respiratory tract, fever, sore throat, lethargy
Prevention: Immunization vaccine

Dysentery
Definition: Infectious disorder characterized by inflammation of the intestines.
Causes: transmission of bacteria through contaminated food and water or by human excrement
Symptoms: Abdominal pain and straining; diarrhea, with bloody or mucus-filled stools
Prevention: Sanitary environment

Smallpox
Definition: Acute, infectious disease caused by a virus and characterized by fever and lesions
Causes: Contact with an infected person
Symptoms: Fever, skin lesions, rash
Prevention: Vaccination

Scarlet Fever
Definition: Acute infectious disease caused by certain types of hemolytic streptococcal bacteria
Causes: Streptococcus pyogenes
Symptoms: Small red spots on skin that become scaly; fever, sore throat, headache, nausea, swollen glands and painful red tongue
Prevention: unknown—treatment is with penicillin or Gamma globulin

Tuberculosis
Definition: An acute disease that affects the respiratory system.

Answer Key continues on page 32.

Continued from page 31.

Causes: bacteria transmitted through the air by coughing or by personal contact with an infected individual; also from infected milk or food
Symptoms: Lethargy, weight loss, persistent cough, sweats, chest pain, and bloody sputum
Prevention: Good hygienic and nutritional conditions, early diagnosis and treatment to minimize spreading

Typhus
Definition: Acute infectious disease characterized by fever, headaches, chills, generalized pain and an accumulation of blood toxins

Causes: transmitted person to person by body lice, fleas, ticks, and mites
Symptoms: Lesions (from bites), fever, chills, headaches, aches and pains along with blood toxins
Prevention: Vaccination and rodent control

Resources

One of the finest, most complete bibliographies of books and videos on the Holocaust is available through:

U.S. Holocaust Memorial Museum
100 Raoul Wallenberg Place, SW
Washington, D.C. 20004
(202-488-0400)

Videos

Auschwitz: If You Cried You Died
Impact America Productions, Inc.

Children in the Holocaust
Phoenix/BFA Films and Video

Kitty—Return to Auschwitz
Anne Frank Center

Genocide, 1941–1945 (A World at War Series)
A&E

The Hangman
CRM

The Holocaust: Turning Point Series
CRM

Lodz Ghetto
Jewish Heritage Project

The Only Way
Social Studies School Services

Persecuted and Forgotten
EBS Productions

Raoul Wallenberg: Between the Lines
Social Studies School Services

Triumph of the Will
Zenger Video

Triumph of Memory
PBS Video

Sources of Videos

A&E Home Video
P.O. Box 2284
South Burlington, VT 05407
(800-423-1212)

Anne Frank Center
106 East 19 St.
New York, NY 10003
(212-529-9532)

CRM
2215 Faraday, Suite F
Carlsbad, CA 92008
(800-421-0833)

EBS Productions
330 Ritch Street
San Francisco, CA 94107
(415-495-2327

Impact America Foundations Inc.
1900 Keystone Crossing, Suite 390
Indianapolis, IN 46240
(317-848-5134)

Jewish Heritage Project, Inc.
150 Franklin St., #1W
New York, NY 10003
(212-925-9067)

PBS Videos
1320 Braddock Pl.
Alexandria, VA 22314
(800-344-3337)

Phoenix/BFA /Films and Video
2349 Chaffee Dr.
St. Louis, MO 63146
(314-569-0211)

Social Studies School Services
10200 Jefferson Blvd., Room J.
P.O. Box 802
Culver City, CA 90232
(800-421-4246)

Zenger Video
10200 Jefferson Blvd., Room 202
P.O. Box 802
Culver City, CA 90232
(800-421-4246)